To:_____

From:_____

Date:_____

Cheerful looks make every dish
a feast, and it is that
which crowns a welcome.

PHILIP MASSINGER

With Love from a
COUNTRY KITCHEN

Best of Show

Pickles

Peach Marmalade

Blueberry Jam

Paintings by **Deb Strain**

HARVEST HOUSE PUBLISHERS
EUGENE, OREGON

This book is dedicated to Finnigan and Graham,
our first two grandchildren,
who light up our world every day.

With Love from a Country Kitchen

Artwork copyright © 2014 by Deb Strain by arrangement with Penny Lane Publishing, Inc. Artwork may not be copied or reproduced without permission. For more information regarding artwork featured in this book, please contact:

Penny Lane Publishing, Inc.
(800) 273-5263
info@pennylanepublishing.com

Published by Harvest House Publishers
Eugene, Oregon 97402
www.harvesthousepublishers.com

ISBN 978-0-7369-5877-6

Design and production by Katie Brady Design, Eugene, Oregon

Harvest House Publishers has made every effort to trace the ownership of all poems and quotes. In the event of a question arising from the use of a poem or quote, we regret any error made and will be pleased to make the necessary correction in future editions of this book.

All Scripture verses are taken from the New King James Version. Copyright © 1982 by Thomas Nelson, Inc. Used by permission. All rights reserved.

Printed in China.

13 14 15 16 17 18 19 20 21 / IM / 10 9 8 7 6 5 4 3 2 1

Country Kitchen Recipes

ORGANIC
Milk
100%
Natural

Sweet April
showers do spring
May flowers.
THOMAS TUSSER

Recipes
for **Spring**

Is it so small a thing
To have enjoyed the sun,
To have lived light
in the spring,
To have loved, to have
thought, to have done.
MATTHEW ARNOLD

Recipes from Home ~

For the LORD is good;
His mercy is everlasting;
And His truth endures
to all generations.

THE BOOK OF PSALMS

The pleasure of love is in loving.

FRANCOIS DE LA ROCHEFOUCAULD

Where did you come from, baby dear?
Out of the everywhere into the here.

GEORGE MacDONALD

Blessed is the influence
of one true, loving
human soul on another.

GEORGE ELIOT

A laugh, to be joyous, must flow
from a joyous heart, for without
kindness, there can be no true joy.

THOMAS CARLYLE

Home is the one place in all this world where
hearts are sure of each other. It is the place
of confidence. It is the place where we tear
off that mask of guarded and suspicious
coldness which the world forces us to wear
in self-defense, and where we pour out
the unreserved communications of
full and confiding hearts. It is the spot
where expressions of tenderness gush out
without any sensation of awkwardness
and without any dread of ridicule.

Behave so the aroma
of your actions may
enhance the general
sweetness of the
atmosphere.

HENRY DAVID THOREAU

FREDERICK W. ROBERTSON

5

Recipe

Cherry Cheesecake Cups

2 (8-ounce) packages cream
    cheese
¾ cup sugar
2 eggs

1 tablespoon lemon juice
1 teaspoon vanilla
20-25 vanilla wafers
1 (21-ounce) can cherry pie filling

Combine all ingredients except the vanilla wafers and pie filling and beat with an electric mixer for 5 minutes. Place cupcake liners in muffin pans. Set one vanilla wafer in the bottom of each liner and then fill each liner 2/3 full with cheesecake mixture. Bake at 375 degrees for 15 minutes. (Note that the filling will not look brown.) Cool and top with cherry pie filling.

Recipe

Everyone's Favorite Broccoli Salad

1 bunch broccoli, cut into small pieces
    (peel stems first)
½ pound raisins
½ pound bacon, cooked and crumbled
1 (8-ounce) can water chestnuts, sliced
½ onion, chopped
1 cup diced celery

Dressing
1 cup mayonnaise
⅓ cup sugar
1 teaspoon vinegar or
    lemon juice

Combine all salad ingredients and set aside. In a small bowl, mix all the dressing ingredients together. Just before serving, stir the dressing, pour it over the salad, and mix well.

Recipes from Home ~

Melinda's Quiche Lorraine

1 (9-inch) unbaked pie crust
8 slices bacon
4 green onions, chopped
2 cups Swiss cheese, shredded and divided
6 large eggs
1 cup heavy cream
$\frac{1}{2}$ teaspoon salt
$\frac{1}{8}$ teaspoon ground red pepper
$\frac{1}{8}$ teaspoon ground white pepper
$\frac{1}{8}$ teaspoon nutmeg

Bake pie crust at 400 degrees for 7 minutes. Remove from oven and set aside. Cook bacon until crisp. Drain and crumble it. Sprinkle the bacon, green onions, and 1 cup of cheese onto the baked pie crust. In a medium mixing bowl, whisk together eggs and next 4 ingredients. Pour the mixture onto the crust. Sprinkle with the remaining 1 cup of cheese and nutmeg. Bake at 350 degrees for 40 minutes or until set. Let stand 10 minutes before serving.

Katie's Favorite Coffee Cake

3 cups flour
½ cup shortening
2 tablespoons baking powder
2 eggs
½ teaspoon salt
1 cup milk
1½ cups sugar

In a large mixing bowl, blend the flour, salt, shortening, milk, baking powder, sugar, and eggs with a fork. Pour half the batter into a greased 10 x 14-inch pan.

Topping

2 cups brown sugar
½ cup melted butter
2 ½ tablespoons cinnamon
½ cup flour

Mix the topping ingredients until crumbly. Spoon half of the topping mixture over batter, covering as much of the batter as possible. Repeat layers with remaining batter and topping. Bake at 375 degrees for 25-30 minutes. Insert a fork or wooden pick into the middle of the cake to make sure it is done.

A woman's whole life is a history of the affections.

WASHINGTON IRVING

Home is the resort
Of love, of joy, of peace and plenty, where,
Supporting and supported, polish'd friends,
And dear relations mingle into bliss.

JAMES THOMSON

Not life, but good life, is to be chiefly valued.

SOCRATES

We are shaped and fashioned by what we love.

JOHANN WOLFGANG VON GOETHE

Laughter is brightest where food is best.

IRISH PROVERB

Life is made up, not of great sacrifices or duties, but of little things in which smiles and kindness, and small obligations, given habitually, are what win and preserve the heart and secure comfort.

SIR H. DAVY

Frame your mind to mirth and merriment, which bars a thousand harms and lengthens life.

WILLIAM SHAKESPEARE

Blest be those feasts with simple plenty crown'd, Where all the ruddy family around Laugh at the jests or pranks that never fail, Or sigh with pity at some mournful tale.

OLIVER GOLDSMITH

You are as welcome as flowers in May.

CHARLES MACKLIN

The cheerful live longest in years, and afterwards in our regards. Cheerfulness is the off-shoot of goodness.

CHRISTIAN NESTELL BOVEE

I love these little people; and it is not a slight thing, when they, who are so fresh from God, love us.

CHARLES DICKENS

The happiest moments of my life have been the few which I have passed at home in the bosom of my family.

THOMAS JEFFERSON

Blessed be the hand that prepares a pleasure for a child, for there is no saying when and where it may bloom forth.

DOUGLAS WILLIAM JERROLD

Recipes for **Summer**

A bird sang sweet and strong
In the top of the highest tree,
He said, "I pour out my
     heart in song
For the summer that soon
     shall be."

GEORGE WILLIAM CURTIS

There is an invisible
garment woven around us from
our earliest years; it is made of the
way we eat, the way we walk, the
way we greet people.

JEAN GIRAUDOUX

A garden of God is our childhood, each day
A festival with laughter and play,
And angels of peace gather there in the glen,
And tiptoe on carpets of flowers, and then
Joy, glee and frolic and innocent fun—
These are the blossoms that smile at the sun.

MICAH JOSEPH LEBENSOHN

Who is not attracted by
right and pleasant children
to prattle, to creep, and to
play with them?

EPICTETUS

We need love's tender lessons taught
As only weakness can;
God hath His small interpreters;
The child must teach the man.

JOHN GREENLEAF WHITTIER

15

Mom's Creeping Crust Cobbler

¼ cup butter or margarine
1 cup flour
1½ cups sugar, more or less, divided
1 teaspoon baking powder

½ cup milk
2 cups fruit, fresh or canned
  (any kind will do)
instant tapioca or cornstarch, optional

Heat oven to 350 degrees. Melt butter in an 8 x 8-inch pan in the oven. In a mixing bowl, combine the flour, 1 cup sugar, and baking powder with a fork. Add the milk to the dry mixture and mix to form sticky dough. Drop dough by spoonfuls into the melted butter. Using a saucepan on medium heat, cook the fruit and about ½ cup sugar (if using canned, sweetened fruit, this can be omitted; simply heat), adjusting the amount of sugar according to the sweetness of fruit. If the fruit mixture is too juicy, you can add a spoonful of instant tapioca or cornstarch to thicken it, but this isn't necessary. Pour fruit mixture over dough and bake for 30-35 minutes or until golden brown.

Fresh Strawberry and Spinach Salad

1 pound baby spinach, rinsed and drained
1 pint fresh strawberries, hulled and sliced

½ cup chopped pecans

Tear spinach into smaller pieces and toss together with strawberries and pecans in a large salad bowl.

Dressing:

⅓ cup gourmet wine vinegar
¼ teaspoon salt
½ cup sugar
1 teaspoon dry mustard

1 tablespoon dry onions
1 teaspoon poppy seeds
¾ cup oil

Mix dressing ingredients well, adding the oil last. Just before serving, pour dressing over salad and toss lightly.

Recipe

Picnic Perfect Pasta Salad

1 (16-ounce) box penne rigate pasta, cooked
   and drained
¼-½ bottle Italian salad dressing
Your favorite cut or diced fresh vegetables (tomatoes,
   broccoli, cauliflower, green peppers, carrots, etc.)
½ cup shredded cheddar cheese

Cook pasta according to the directions on the
package. When done, drain, rinse with cool water,
and drain again; allow the pasta to cool. Stir
together the cooled pasta and vegetables. Pour
the dressing on top, add the shredded cheese,
and gently stir until mixed well. Chill at least 1
hour. As the salad chills, the pasta will absorb the
dressing, so you may need to add a little more
before serving.

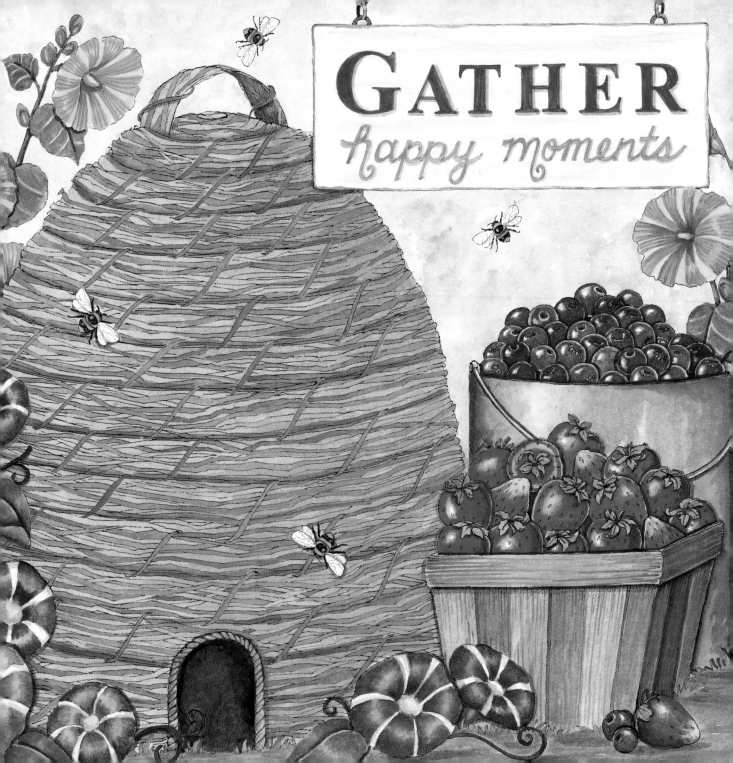

The only gift is
a portion of thyself.

RALPH WALDO EMERSON

A little child, a limber elf,
Singing, dancing to itself,
A fairy thing with red round cheeks
That always finds, and never seeks.

SAMUEL TAYLOR COLERIDGE

How dear to this heart are
the scenes of my childhood,
when fond recollection
presents them to view!

SAMUEL WOODWORTH

What greater thing is there
for two human souls than
to feel that they are joined
for life—to strengthen each
other in all labor, to rest on
each other in all sorrow.

GEORGE ELIOT

Love needs new leaves
every summer of life.

HARRIET BEECHER STOWE

Cheerfulness keeps up a kind of daylight in the mind, filling it with a steady and perpetual serenity.

JOSEPH ADDISON

Show me another pleasure like dinner which comes every day and lasts an hour.

CHARLES MAURICE DE TALLEYRAND

Divine love is a sacred flower, which in its early bud is happiness, and in its full bloom is heaven.

JAMES HERVEY

One can say everything best over a meal.

GEORGE ELIOT

The heart hath its own memory, like the mind, and in it are enshrined the precious keepsakes, into which is wrought the giver's loving thought.

HENRY WADSWORTH LONGFELLOW

Recipes for Autumn

The tints of autumn—
a mighty flower garden
blossoming under the spell
of the enchanter, frost.

JOHN GREENLEAF WHITTIER

*Home is the sacred
refuge of our life.*

JOHN DRYDEN

A mother's heart is always
with her children.

JEWISH PROVERB

Cheerful looks make every
dish a feast, and it is that
which crowns a welcome.

PHILIP MASSINGER

*The art of dining well is no
slight art, the pleasure not a
slight pleasure.*

MICHEL DE MONTAIGNE

Home is the sphere of
harmony and peace,
the spot where angels find
a resting place,
when bearing blessings,
they descend to earth.

SARAH JOSEPHA HALE

No matter what you've done for yourself
or for humanity, if you can't look back
on having given love and attention to
your own family, what have you really
accomplished?

ELBERT HUBBARD

Peace to this house.

THE BOOK OF LUKE

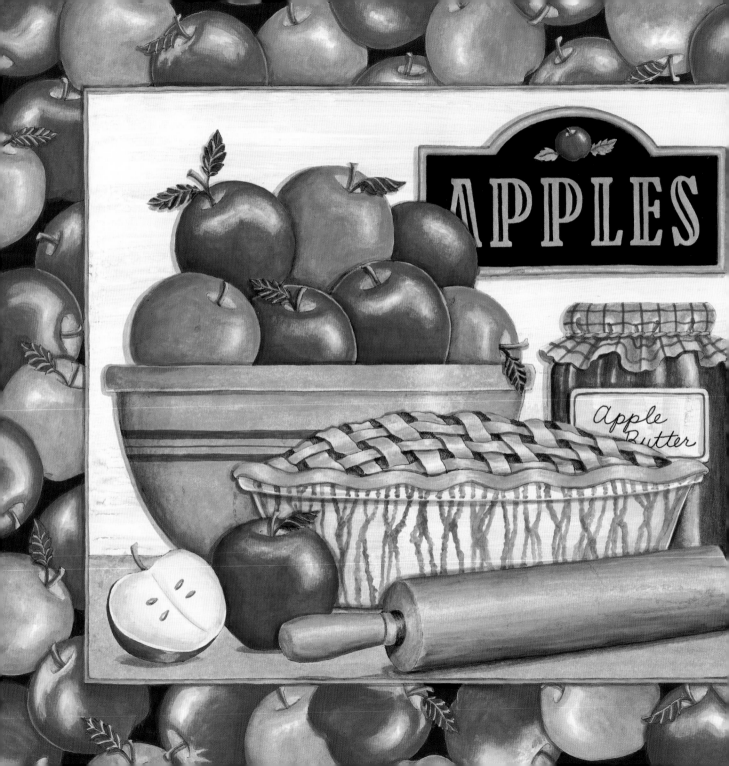

Recipe

Welcome-to-Fall Apple Crisp

3-4 medium apples
1/2 cup quick-cooking oatmeal
1/2 cup brown sugar
1/3 cup flour
1/3 cup butter
1 teaspoon cinnamon

Pare, core, and thinly slice the apples and place
the slices in a greased 8 x 8-inch baking pan.
Combine the remaining ingredients, mix well,
and sprinkle the mixture over the apples. Bake
35-40 minutes at 350 degrees.

Recipe
Sour Cream Potatoes

1 (2-pound) package frozen hash browns
1 cup chopped onions
1 (10 ¾-ounce) can cream of chicken soup
2 cups sour cream
½ cup butter or margarine, melted
1 cup sharp cheddar cheese, shredded
salt and pepper to taste

Mix all ingredients well. Pour into a 9 x 13-inch pan and bake at 350 degrees for 1 hour.

Recipe
Sweet, Sweet Potato Casserole

2 large (32-ounce) cans
sweet potatoes, drained
1½ cups sugar
2 eggs

1½ teaspoons vanilla
⅓-½ cup milk
½ cup butter, melted

Using a mixer, combine all ingredients and then pour into a greased 9 x 13-inch baking dish.

Topping

¾ cup oatmeal
3 tablespoons flour
¾ cup brown sugar

1½ teaspoon
cinnamon
⅓ cup butter, melted

1 cup crushed pecans
mini marshmallows

Stir together all topping ingredients except the marshmallows until large crumbles form. Sprinkle crumbled mixture over the filling. Bake uncovered at 350 degrees for 25 minutes. Remove from oven, sprinkle mini marshmallows on the top, and bake an additional 5 minutes.

Recipe
Take-Along Turketti

8 ounces dry spaghetti
2 cups turkey or chicken, cooked and cut up
¼ cup green pepper, chopped (optional)
½ small onion, chopped
1 (14-ounce) can chicken broth

1 (10 ¾-ounce) can cream of
   mushroom soup
½ teaspoon salt
½ teaspoon pepper
½ pound cheese, grated

Break the spaghetti into 2-inch pieces and cook in a large pot of lightly salted boiling water for about 12 minutes. Drain well. Stir soup, salt, and pepper into hot chicken broth. Add cooked spaghetti and all remaining ingredients except ½ cup cheese, mix well, and then pour into a lightly greased 9 x 13-inch baking dish. Sprinkle remaining cheese on top, cover, and bake at 350 degrees for 25 minutes. Remove the cover and bake another 20 minutes.

Recipe
Celebration Caramel Corn

1 (7-ounce) bag hull-less popcorn, popped
½ cup butter or margarine
1 cup brown sugar

Melt butter and brown sugar together in a small pan over medium heat or in the microwave. Pour the popcorn into a large bowl and then pour the butter and brown sugar mixture over the popcorn. Stir well so that no mixture is left in the bottom of the bowl.

Pour the mixture onto a cookie sheet with a rim and bake at 250 degrees for 8 minutes. Remove from the oven and stir the mixture. Bake another 8 minutes and stir again. Bake a final 8 minutes, remove from oven, and pour mixture onto waxed paper to cool, stirring occasionally to break up the clumps. Store in a gallon-sized plastic food storage bag.

Bricks and mortar make a house, but the laughter of children makes a home.

IRISH PROVERB

Sit down and feed, and welcome to our table.

WILLIAM SHAKESPEARE

But what on earth is half so dear—so longed for—as the hearth of home?

EMILY BRONTË

A cheerful mind is a vigorous mind.

JEAN DE LA FONTAINE

Trust in the LORD, and do good;
Dwell in the land, and feed on His faithfulness.
Delight yourself also in the LORD,
And He shall give you the desires of your heart.

THE BOOK OF PSALMS

You do not really understand something unless you can explain it to your grandmother.

PROVERB

Happiness seems made to be shared.

PIERRE CORNEILLE

It is a rare and difficult attainment to grow old gracefully and happily.

LYDIA MARIA FRANCIS CHILD

To love, and be loved, is the greatest happiness of existence.

SYDNEY SMITH

A house without love may be a castle, or a palace, but it is not a home; love is the life of a true home.

JOHN LUBBOCK

Truths are first clouds; then rain, then harvest and food.

HENRY WARD BEECHER

I had rather be on my farm than be emperor of the world.

GEORGE WASHINGTON

There never was any heart truly great and generous, that was not also tender and compassionate.

ROBERT SOUTH

Every house where Love abides, and Friendship is a guest, is surely home, and home-sweet-home: for there the heart can rest.

HENRY VAN DYKE

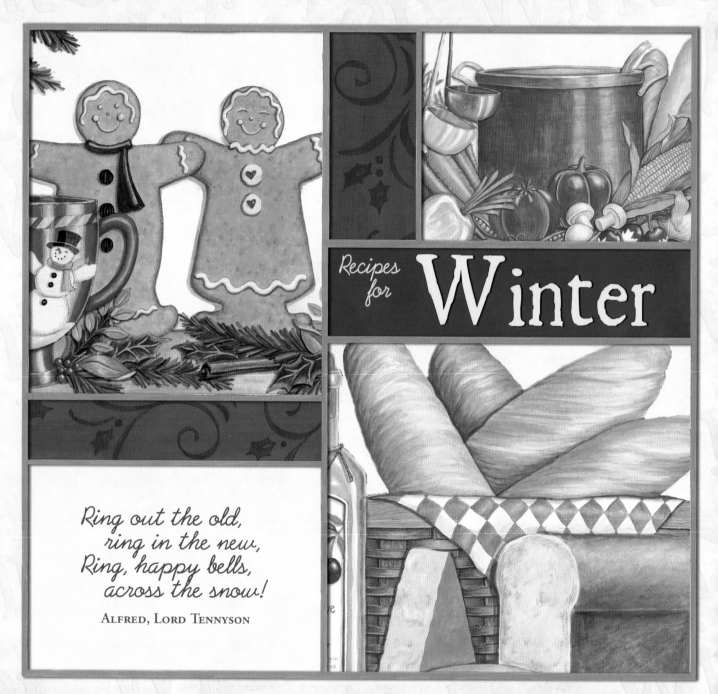

Recipes for Winter

Ring out the old,
ring in the new,
Ring, happy bells,
across the snow!

ALFRED, LORD TENNYSON

Sit with me at the homestead hearth,
And stretch the hands of memory forth
To warm them at the wood-fire's blaze.

JOHN GREENLEAF WHITTIER

Christmas! 'Tis the
season for kindling the
fire of hospitality in the
hall, the genial fire of
charity in the heart.

WASHINGTON IRVING

In all ranks of life the
human heart yearns for the
beautiful; and the beautiful
things that God makes are
his gift to all alike.

HARRIET BEECHER STOWE

Over the river, and through the wood—
when Grandmother sees us come,
she will say, "O, dear, the children are here,
bring pie for everyone."

LYDIA MARIA CHILD, FROM "OVER THE RIVER AND THROUGH THE WOOD"

A house is built of logs and stone,
Of tiles and posts and piers,
A home is built of loving deeds
That stand a thousand years.

VICTOR HUGO

Merry-Christmas-Morning Ham and Cheddar Hash Brown Bake

3 cups frozen, shredded hash brown potatoes, thawed
⅓ cup butter, melted
1 cup cooked, diced ham
1 cup shredded cheddar cheese
¼ cup green pepper, chopped (optional)
2 eggs
½ cup milk
salt and pepper to taste

Press hash browns between paper towels to remove moisture, and then press into the bottom and up the sides of an ungreased 9-inch round baking pan. Drizzle with melted butter. Bake at 425 degrees for 25 minutes. Combine ham, cheese, and green pepper and spoon the mixture onto the baked crust. In a small bowl, beat the eggs, milk, salt, and pepper. Pour this over the ham mixture. Bake at 350 degrees for 25 minutes.

'Tis not the food, but the content,
That makes the table's merriment.

ROBERT HERRICK

Children are the hands by
which we take hold of heaven.

HENRY WARD BEECHER

I get but sounds and odors sweet
Who can wonder I love to stay,
Week after week, here hidden away,
In this sly nook that I love the best—
This little brown house like a
ground-bird's nest?

ELLA WHEELER WILCOX

Small cheer and great
welcome makes a merry feast.

WILLIAM SHAKESPEARE

Worries go down better
with soup than without.

Jewish Proverb

The smallest seed of faith is
better than the largest fruit of
happiness.

Henry David Thoreau

Every day they continued to
meet together...They broke
bread in their homes and ate
together with glad and sincere
hearts.

The Book of Acts

Her pleasures are in the happiness
of her family.

Jean Jacques Rousseau

Sweet is the hour that brings us home,
Where all will spring to meet us;
Where hands are striving, as we come,
To be the first to greet us.

Eliza Cook

Recipe

Our Favorite Weeknight, Super Easy, Cheese Soup

1 (10 ¾-ounce) can cheddar cheese soup
1 (10 ¾-ounce) can cream of broccoli soup
1 (10 ¾-ounce) can cream of potato soup
1 (15-ounce) can diced potatoes, drained
3 soup cans milk
¼-½ cup shredded cheddar cheese
Extras: diced ham, onions, tomatoes, bacon, steamed broccoli,
   or anything that sounds good!

Pour each can of soup into a large pot. Add drained
potatoes and 3 soup cans of milk. Stir until well
blended. Simmer over low heat, stirring often. Add
shredded cheese and any extras. Continue to heat
until the cheese has melted.

Recipe

Grandma's Best Zucchini Bread

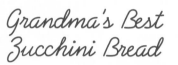

Dry Ingredients:
3 ¼ cups flour
3 cups sugar
2 teaspoons baking soda
1½ teaspoons salt
1 teaspoon nutmeg
1 teaspoon ground
   cinnamon

Wet Ingredients:
1 cup canola oil
4 eggs, beaten
⅔ cup water
2 cups grated zucchini
1 teaspoon lemon juice

Mix dry ingredients in a large bowl and set aside. In a separate bowl, beat together wet ingredients. Fold this mixture into the dry ingredients and mix well. Pour the batter evenly into two greased and floured loaf pans. Bake at 350 degrees for 1 hour or until done in the middle when tested with a wooden toothpick. Cool for 10 minutes and then remove from pans.

Olive
Oil

Extra Virgin
Cold Press
16 oz

When love and skill work together, expect a masterpiece.

JOHN RUSKIN

That day is lost on which one has not laughed.

FRENCH PROVERB

Our home joys are the most delightful earth affords, and the joy of parents in their children is the most holy joy of humanity.

JOHANN HEINRICH PESTALOZZI

A joy shared is a joy doubled.

JOHANN WOLFGANG VON GOETHE

Our natural and happiest life is when we lose ourselves in the exquisite absorption of home.

DINAH MARIA MULOCK

So of cheerfulness, or a good temper, the more it is spent, the more it remains.

RALPH WALDO EMERSON

Our
Family Favorites

Our Family Favorites

_____

_____

_____

_____

_____

_____

_____

_____

_____

_____

Our Family Favorites

_____

_____

_____

_____

_____

_____

_____

_____

_____

_____

Our Family Favorites

Our Family Favorites

_____

_____

_____

_____

_____

_____

_____

_____

_____

_____

_____

_____

So the short journey came blithely to an end, and in the twilight she saw a group of loving faces at the door of a humble little house, which was more beautiful than any palace in her eyes, for it was home.

LOUISA MAY ALCOTT, FROM *AN OLD-FASHIONED GIRL*